Catholics
Why We Do What We Do

By
Heather Fleming

~ Dedication ~

To the Most Sacred Heart of Jesus.
I am in awe of Thy Mercy!

Special Thanks to
My parents, Jack & Doreen; my loving husband, Sean and
our beautiful children: Kayla, Raelin, Liam,
Jacinta, Riley, and Allyson.
Thank you for all your love and encouragement!

~ Table of Contents ~

Dedication

Introduction

The Eucharist

Magisterium

The Mass

The Crucifix

Honoring Mary

The Angels & Saints

Purgatory

The Rapture or Not

The Church & Her Imagery

Rote Prayers

Baptizing Our Babies

My Conclusion

Catholic Prayers

Resources

~ Introduction ~

What makes Catholics so different from other denominations? Why do many denominations almost have a hatred or misunderstanding toward Catholics? It seems some know more about why they are not Catholic than why they are the denomination they are.

Over the past 15 years or so, I've encountered various Protestants (or non-Catholics) who have questioned me... ok, drilled me on my Catholic faith. As a cradle Catholic, I did not know why we do much of the things we do. Our Faith Formation programs do not dive very deep into our Catholic faith. Faith Formation programs are there to get children their sacraments. Unfortunately, a good percentage of parents also do not know why they are Catholic or why their children need these sacraments. Many do it because it's a tradition in their family and there is an obligation to do so.

I put this book together for both Catholics, non-Catholics, and Protestants. For the Catholic -- like I was -- who doesn't really know why they are Catholic; for the non-Catholic who is curious about the Catholic faith; and for the Protestant who presumes they know Catholics are blasphemous heathens that are going to hell because of their abominations. I hope this will help make things clearer to you all.

All of the **bold** text throughout the book are verses from the bible. I also added a few paragraphs from the Catechism of the Catholic Church at the end of each chapter pertaining to that specific subject. I invite you to read them (each paragraph is numbered according to the CCC). They are written with such faith and wisdom. There is not a lot of my opinion in this book. It is a book I put together from a few of the studies and some of the books I've read over the years.

One more thing I would like to say about this book. It is not about the politics of the Catholic church. **"Let the weeds grow with the wheat."** Catholics know there are weeds in many places in our church at this moment in time, and other moments in history for that matter, but our faith is about sticking to the true church Jesus Christ established on earth with His apostles as the foundation. Good and bad come and go. Even Jesus had a betrayer in His inner circle of 12 men, and that betrayer was needed to fulfill His Ultimate Glory. God knows His betrayers and we just have to pray for discernment and continue to pray for them.

I'd like to say a quick prayer before we get started: Heavenly Father, please send Your Holy Spirit down upon the readers of this book. May they receive discernment in these pages for a clearer understanding of the Catholic faith. I ask this in the Name of Your Son, Our Lord Jesus Christ. Amen.

~ The Eucharist ~

"Do this in remembrance of Me..."
The Eucharist is the Source and Summit of the Catholic Faith

We believe our priests consecrate bread and wine into the Body and Blood, Soul, and Divinity of Jesus Christ every time we celebrate mass. It is a Eucharistic Celebration, and this is the very reason why many of our churches are adorned with such magnificence.

<u>Did the Apostles Partake in the Eucharist</u>

History tells us that one of the many reasons for Christians being persecuted under Emperor Nero was because Christians were considered "cannibals."

Two of the reasons for Christians were persecuted in Rome were: Thyestian banquets and Oedipodean intercourse, which is cannibalism and incest. Cannibalism because they would eat the Flesh and Blood of Jesus Christ, and incest because they called each other "brother and sister."

Sts. Peter and Paul were both martyred under Nero. So that places the apostles alive in the timeline of the Eucharist.

Sts. Peter and Paul were partakers of the mass and the consecration of the Host, the Eucharist. This places the mass and consecration in the catacombs of the 1st Century when Rome was still persecuting Christians.

<u>And the Word was Made Flesh</u>

The Body, Blood, Soul, and Divinity of our Lord and Savior Jesus Christ <u>is</u> present in the Tabernacle in our church. The Holy Spirit resides in us, and the Son is physically present in our church. **John 1:14a, "And the Word became flesh and made His dwelling among us."** Many Protestants' interpretation of this verse is, "We consume God's Word (the bible) every day." We believe there are many more references in both the Old and New Testament that refer to our eating -- physically eating His Flesh and I will do my best to point these references out...

<u>Old Testament</u>

<u>The Showbread from the Tabernacle is a Prefigure of Jesus</u>

Rewind to the Old Testament Tabernacle: The Tabernacle in the Desert (**Exodus chapters 36-40**) and King Solomon's Temple (**1 Kings 7:13-51**). A group of Mennonites in Lancaster, Pennsylvania built an exact replica of the Tabernacle as described in extreme detail by God to Moses in the book of Exodus. I had the pleasure of touring it. Upon entering the tent, or "the Dwelling," there is an immediate feeling of being in a Catholic church. It's very quiet, the smell of incense is in the air, candles are lit and there is a sense of sincere reverence just like in a traditional Catholic church.

Solomon's Temple, just like the tent in the desert, had the same items situated in the same places: The lampstand was positioned to the left in the front room, and to the right was the altar which displayed 12 unleavened loaves of bread called "showbread" representing the 12 tribes of Israel. **Exodus 25:30, "On the table you shall always keep showbread set before me."** And straight ahead was the veil which separated the front room from the Holy of Holies which held the Arc of the Covenant. The Trinity is represented in the Old Testament tabernacle: The lampstand, with its tongues of fire, represents the Holy Spirit; the Holy of Holies represents the Father, and the altar with the showbread represents the Son, in which the priests had to eat on a weekly basis.

When entering a Catholic church, there is an altar with the tabernacle behind it. The veil was torn when Jesus died on the cross, so there is no longer a veil that separates us from the Holy of Holies. We enter into the Holy of Holies when we enter our church. (Although, some churches do have curtains in front of the small doors of the tabernacle.) Some churches have the tabernacle off to the side but in most churches, it is centered behind the altar. No matter where the tabernacle is located, a red glassed candle is always lit near it to indicate there is a consecrated host/the True Presence of God in the tabernacle. If the candle is not lit, there is no host present in the Tabernacle. Unless it is a church with a couple of different altars/chapels in different areas of the property, the only time the candle is not lit is on Good Friday when Jesus dies on the cross and so there is no consecrated host.

New Testament

Born in a Manger

From the very first moments of the Man-God's life, He showed He was food. The word "manger" comes from the word manga, which literally means "to eat." The manger is a feed box. The name "Bethlehem" means "The House of Bread," and was also the place where they raised the lambs for the Temple sacrifice.

Do This in Remembrance of Me

Throughout the Old and New Testament, every feast day the Jews celebrated (and still celebrate) was in remembrance of a God moment. When God did something spectacular, or when God was teaching them a lesson out of love. For instance, the Jewish celebrate the Feast of Tabernacles. They pitch tents and live in them for a week for the remembrance of their 40 years in the desert; Shabbat is celebrated every Friday evening at sundown and is the beginning of their Sabbath according to God's law for the Sabbath; Hanukkah for the remembrance of the Maccabean Revolt when they took their Temple back from the Greeks that occupied their city. And of course, the one we still celebrate today in the Messianic Fulfillment, Passover. Mass is our Passover and our Shabbat. By eating His flesh and drinking His blood we are joined in union to receive the joys and splendor of heaven.

The day after He multiplied the loaves and fishes in **John 6:11-13, "When Passover was near." John 6:4, John 6:32-34, "Jesus said to them, 'Amen, amen, I say to you, it was not Moses who gave the bread from heaven; my Father gives you the true bread from heaven. For the bread of God is the bread that which comes down from heaven and gives life to the world.' So they said to Him, 'Sir, give us this bread always.'"** He goes right into His Bread of Life Discourse: **John 6:35-59a, "I am the bread of life. Your ancestors ate the manna in the wilderness, yet they died. But here is the bread that comes down from heaven, which anyone may eat and not die. I am the living bread that came down from heaven. Whoever eats this bread will live forever. This bread is my flesh, which I will give for the life of the world.' Then the Jews began to argue sharply among themselves, 'How can this man** give us his flesh to eat?' Jesus said to them, 'Amen, amen, I tell you, unless you eat the flesh of the Son of Man and drink his blood, you have no life in you. Whoever eats my flesh and drinks my blood has eternal life, and I will raise them up at the last day. <u>For my flesh is true food and my blood is true drink.</u> Whoever eats my flesh and drinks my blood remains in me and I in him. Just as the living Father sent me and I live because of the Father, so the one who feeds on me will have life because of me. This is the bread that came down from heaven. Your ancestors ate manna and died, but whoever feeds on this bread will live forever.'" After this, in **John 6:66**, He allowed many of His followers to leave without any further explanation -- like He typically would after a parable -- saying to them, "this is what I really meant."

John 6:63 "'It is the spirit that gives life, while the flesh is of no avail. The words I have spoken to you are spirit and life.'" Catholics believe when He says this, He is not referring to His own flesh. He is referring to our flesh. It is the Spirit that gives us the understanding needed for the words He spoke. It is through the words and through the Spirit that the priest changes the bread and wine into the Body and Blood of Jesus Christ. He shows His apostles over and over again on what they are to do:

Matthew 26:26-29a, "While they were eating, Jesus took bread, and when he had given thanks, he broke it and gave it to his disciples, saying, 'Take and eat; this is my body.' Then he took a cup, and when he had given thanks, he gave it to them, saying, 'Drink from it, all of you. This is my blood of the covenant, which is poured out for many for the forgiveness of sins.'"

As I mentioned earlier, **John 6:11**, "Then Jesus took the loaves, gave thanks, and distributed them..." and again, John 21:13, "Jesus came over, took the bread and gave it to them, and did the same with the fish."

Luke 24:30-31, "And it happened that while he was with them at table, he took bread, said the blessing, broke it and gave it to them. With that their eyes were opened and they recognized him and he disappeared from their sight."

The first public miracle of Jesus was turning water into wine and the last He turns wine into His Blood every day through the Spirit and the words of the Catholic priest.

Where the Old and New Testament are Joined Together
The Paschal Lamb and the Lamb of God
Paschal Lamb
Exodus 12:5-6, "The animals you choose must be a year-old male <u>without defect</u>, and you may take them

from the sheep or the goats. Take care of them until the fourteenth day of the month, then all the members of the community of Israel must slaughter them at twilight..." Jesus entered the city of Jerusalem as the Jews were bringing their lambs and goat sacrifices to be prepared for the Passover (**John 11:55**) and in **John 19:4, "Once more Pilate went out and said to them, 'Look, I am bringing him out to you, so that you may know that I find no guilt in him'"** See how they are connected? He is our Unblemished Lamb of God. Our Passover meal.

Lamb of God

Another bible reference Catholics connect to the Eucharist: **Genesis 22:2-13** God tells Abraham to **"Take your son Isaac, your only one, whom you love, and go to the land of Moriah. There you shall offer him up as a holocaust on a height that I will point out to you."** When Abraham lays wood on Isaac's shoulders, Isaac asks, **"where is the lamb for the holocaust?"** Abraham replies, **"God Himself will provide the lamb for the holocaust."** Before Abraham sacrifices his son, an angel comes down and stops him. Still, a sacrifice had to be made, so God sent a ram for Abraham's sacrifice. That is a significant connection for us Catholics. Some Protestants say God provided a lamb for Abraham to sacrifice that day. But in fact, **Genesis 22:13,**

"Abraham looked about, he spied a ram caught by its horns in the thicket. So he went and took the ram and offered it up as a holocaust in place of his son." God's Lamb sacrifice had not yet come. And when God's Lamb came, He carried His cross up that same mountain range Isaac carried the wood. The hill Golgotha (**John 19:17**) was on Mount Moriah -- 300 meters from the Temple (**2 Chronicles 3:1**).

Ecce Agnus Dei (Behold the Lamb of God)

"Host" means victim. The Eucharist is also called the Host. Jesus is our Paschal Lamb. Every day at mass the priest repeats the words of Jesus during the Last Supper when the priest takes the bread and wine and consecrates it into the Body, Blood, Soul, and Divinity of Jesus Christ. After he consecrates the host, the priest says, **John 1:29b, "'Behold, the Lamb of God,' Behold Him who takes away the sin of the world."** Rev. 19:9, **"Blessed are those who are called to the Supper of the Lamb."** Then we respond with the words of the Centurion, **"Lord I am not worthy that You should enter under my roof, but only say the words and my soul shall be healed."**

What Changes[1]

"We believe that a complete change takes place in the elements offered to God in the Mass. What were bread and wine become Jesus's Body and Blood. Theologians call this change transubstantiation -- a change in the very substance. That is why Catholics usually prefer not to refer to the consecrated gifts as "bread" and "wine." Sometimes they will refer to the "host" (using an ancient sacrificial term) for the species of bread and "the Precious Blood" to refer to the contents of the chalice. But in either species, Christ is entirely and truly present."

<u>Eucharistic Adoration</u>

Because we believe the priest transforms the bread and wine into the Body and Blood of Jesus Christ, the eucharist is the "source and summit" of the Catholic faith. It supersedes everything else. It is the center and the highest point of our faith. Nothing is higher than the consecrated host of Our Lord and Savior.

In a local Catholic parish near you, I invite you to look on their website to see if and when they offer "Eucharistic

---

[1] "What Changes" excerpted from "Faith Charts: The Mass at a Glance" by Mike Aquilina ©Our Sunday Visitor. Used by permission, no other use of this material is authorized.

Adoration." If your parish is blessed with a perpetual adoration chapel -- meaning there is a designated chapel that has the Eucharist exposed all day every day -- even better! But most parishes will offer at the very least an hour of adoration on the first Friday of every month.

Adoration is a time to go into the church and sit in the Lord's Presence with the Host/Eucharist exposed on the altar in a monstrance. It is a very quiet, personal, and intimate time with our Lord Jesus Christ. If you have never been in a Catholic Church before, going to adoration would be the best time to get acquainted. No one will bother you. It's just you and Jesus. In Adoration, we do our best to settle our minds in order to become still in His Presence.

Miracles of the Eucharist

There are countless miracles that have happened and many are still living, bleeding flesh on display today. The scientific evidence that comes back from the testing labs is incredible! Many of the bleeding Eucharist miracles that are tested by scientists come back to show the tissue sample is heart tissue. And the amazing thing that baffles the scientists is the sample shows the person was still alive when the sample was taken and the person was experiencing extreme trauma due to the amount of white blood cells present in the sample.

What the Catechism says:

"**Do this in memory of me**" CCC 1341: The command of Jesus to repeat His actions and words "**until He comes**" does not only ask us to remember Jesus and what He did. It is directed at the liturgical celebration, by the apostles and their successors, of the memorial of Christ, of His life, of His death, of His Resurrection, and of His intercession in the presence of the Father.

CCC 1342: From the beginning the Church has been faithful to the Lord's command. Of the Church of Jerusalem, it is written:

They devoted themselves to the apostles' teaching and fellowship, to the breaking of bread and the prayers... Day by day, attending the temple together and breaking bread in their homes, they partook of food with glad and generous hearts. (Acts 2:42)

CCC 1344: Thus, from celebration to celebration, as they proclaim the Paschal mystery of Jesus "until He comes," the pilgrim People of God advances, "following the narrow way of the cross," toward the heavenly banquet, when all the elect will be seated at the table of the kingdom.

Catechism Cont'd:

THE LITURGICAL CELEBRATION OF THE EUCHARIST

The Mass of all ages CCC 1345: As early as the second century we have the witness of St. Justin Martyr for the basic lines of the order of the Eucharistic celebration. They have stayed the same until our own day for all the great liturgical families. St. Justin wrote to the pagan emperor Antoninus Pius (138 - 161) around the year 155, explaining what Christians did:

On the day we call the day of the sun, all who dwell in the city or country gather in the same place. The memoirs of the apostles and the writings of the prophets are read, as much as time permits. When the reader has finished, he who presides over those gathered admonishes and challenges them to imitate these beautiful things. Then we all rise together and offer prayers* for ourselves... and for all others, wherever they may be, so that we may be found righteous by our life and actions, and faithful to the commandments, so as to obtain eternal salvation. When the prayers are concluded we exchange the kiss. Then someone brings bread and a cup of water and wine mixed together to him who presides over the brethren. He takes and offers praise and glory to the Father of the universe, through the name of the Son and of the Holy Spirit and for the considerable time he gives thanks (in Greek: Eucharistian) that we have been judged worthy of these gifts. When he has concluded the prayers and thanksgiving, all present give voice to an acclamation by saying: "Amen."

When he who presides has given thanks and the people have responded, those whom we call deacons give to those present the "Eucharisted" bread, wine and water and take them to those who are absent. (St. Justin, Apol. 1, 65-67: PG 6, 428-429; the text before the asterisk (*) is from chap. 67.)

~ Magisterium ~

All of God's creation has a hierarchy. The angels have a hierarchy. There are angels, Archangels, Seraphim and Cherubim, Guardian Angels, etc. They all have their own positions and duties in the heavens and on earth. There is a hierarchy in everything God created. There is order in all of God's creation.

Exodus 18:25-26, "He [Moses] picked out able men from all Israel and put them in charge of the people as officers over groups of thousands, of hundreds, of fifties, and of tens. They rendered decisions for the people in all ordinary cases. The more difficult cases they referred to Moses, but all the lesser cases they settled themselves."

"Able men" in verse 25 were **"able and God-fearing men, trustworthy men who hate dishonest gain," Exodus 18:21a**

Exodus 28: 2-5, **"For the glorious adornment of your brother Aaron you shall have sacred vestments made. Therefore, to the various expert workmen whom I have endowed with skill, you shall give instructions to make such vestments for Aaron as will set him apart for his sacred service as my priest. These are the vestments they** shall make: a breast-piece, an ephod, a rove, a brocaded tunic, a miter and a sash. In making these sacred vestments which your brother Aaron and his sons are to wear in serving as my priests, they shall use gold, violet, purple and scarlet yarn and fine linen."

Exodus 28:40-41, "Likewise, for the glorious adornment of Aaron's sons you shall have tunics and sashes and turbans made. With these you shall clothe your brother Aaron and his sons. Anoint them and ordain them, consecrating them as my priests." God wants His priests to be ordained, consecrated and set apart from the common people.

Hierarchy in the New Testament

Matthew 16:17-19 "Jesus said to him in reply, 'Blessed are you, Simon son of Jonah. For flesh and blood has not revealed this to you, but My heavenly Father. And so I say to you that you are Peter, and upon this rock I will build My church; and the gates of the netherworld shall not prevail against it. I will give you the keys to the kingdom of heaven; and whatever you bind on earth shall be bound in heaven, and whatever you loose on earth shall be loosed in heaven.'" We believe Jesus made Peter the first Pope, and here is where Jesus established authority among His 12 apostles. Only Peter received the keys. Good and bad popes will come and go but as Jesus says, **"the gates of the netherworld shall not prevail against it."** The Catholic Church will have its highs and lows but it will never be destroyed because it is the church Jesus established here on earth.

Filling Judas' seat was the very first thing the apostles did after Jesus' Ascension. **Acts 1:24-26 "Then they prayed and said, 'You, Lord, who know the hearts of all men, show which one of these two You have chosen to occupy this ministry and apostleship from which Judas turned aside to go to his own place.' And they drew lots for them, and the lot fell to Matthias; and he was added to the eleven apostles."** If the 12 were just as ordinary as all other believers, why did they need to fill Judas' seat immediately after Jesus' Ascension? Further, why was it so important to fill the 12th seat if Jesus did not seek to establish a hierarchy/magisterium in His church?

Paul and Barnabas go back to Jerusalem to seek guidance and wisdom from the 12 apostles: **Acts 15:2 "And when Paul and Barnabas had great dissension and debate with them, the brethren determined that Paul and Barnabas and some others of them should go up to Jerusalem to the apostles and elders concerning this issue."** Also, Acts 15:22, **"Then it seemed good to the apostles and the elders, with the whole church, to choose men from** among them to send to Antioch with Paul and Barnabas- Judas called Barsabbas, and Silas, leading men among the brethren..."** Some may say, "This scripture states 'with the whole church,' so it shows the church/the people having authority." I would say then, the apostles and elders would not have been mentioned separately, clearly with more authority, than "the church."

Here the apostles choose the first deacons: **Acts 6:5-6, "The statement found approval with the whole congregation; and they chose Stephen, a man full of faith and of the Holy Spirit, and Philip, Nicanor, Timon, Parmenas and Nicolas, a proselyte from Antioch. And these they brought before the apostles; and after praying, they laid hands on them."** Paul tells Timothy what kind of man a bishop and deacon should be in **1 Timothy 3** and again in **Titus 1:7-9**

Bishops and priests are successors of the apostles by the Order of Melchizedek. In fact, our Catholic priests are ordained to '**the Order of Melchizedek**,' who is described as '**Priest of God Most High**.' **Psalm 110** and extensively reflected upon in the **Letter to the Hebrews**. Melchizedek is the first priest mentioned in the Bible, and he offers the sacrifice of bread and wine. Our Catholic priests offer sacrifices of bread and wine, which is now fulfilled in Christ to be His true Body and Blood.

In **Psalm 110:4b, "Like Melchizedek you are a priest forever."** His priesthood continues through our Catholic Priests, offering a sacrifice of bread and wine before God in Heaven every day of the year with the exception of Good Friday.

Matthew 5:17-18 "Do not think that I came to abolish the Law or the Prophets; I did not come to abolish but to fulfill. For truly I say to you, until heaven and earth pass away, not the smallest letter or stroke shall pass from the Law until all is accomplished."

Jesus Warns the Jewish Leaders of the New Magisterium

Matthew 12:1b - 6, "His disciples were hungry and began to pick the heads of grain and eat them. When the Pharisees saw this, they said to Him, 'See, your disciples are doing what is unlawful to do on the sabbath.' He said to them, 'Have you not read what David did when he and his companions were hungry, how he went into the house of God and ate the bread of offering, which neither he nor his companions but only the priests could lawfully eat?' Or have you not read in the law that on the sabbath the priests serving in the temple violate the sabbath and are innocent? I say to you, something greater than the temple is here.'" Catholic interpretation: Jesus refers to David eating the holy bread (**1 Samuel 21:2-7**).

The priest gave him the holy bread he knew David was going to be the new King of Israel. This was Jesus telling the Pharisees a new king is here. THE king. And a new church will replace the old, but not abolish -- to fulfill.

Another passage Jesus refers to the fulfillment, not abolishment, of His new church: **Luke 5:36b-38, "'No one tears a piece from a new cloak to patch an old one. Otherwise, he will tear the new and the piece from it will not match the old cloak. Likewise, no one pours new wine into old wineskins. Otherwise, the new wine will burst the skins, and it will be spilled and the skins will be ruined. Rather, new wine must be poured into fresh wineskins.'"** He is basically putting the Pharisees on notice so-to-speak, that He is about to fulfill the old to establish the new.

What the Catechism says:

CCC 2663: In the living tradition of prayer, each Church proposes to its faithful, according to its historic, social, and cultural context, a language for prayer: words, melodies, gestures, iconography. The Magisterium of the Church has the task of discerning the fidelity of these ways of praying to the tradition of apostolic faith; it is for pastors and catechists to explain their meaning, always in relation to Jesus Christ.

~ The Mass ~

Candles, and Incense, and Vestments, oh my!

Both Pagan and Jew have always had tradition and rituals in their religion. All 12 apostles were Jewish. They would not have been so quick to fall away from their customs. There has to be some sort of order. Some sort of repetitious ceremony. God created everything with order. Remember, Jesus did not come to abolish, He came to fulfill. If you have ever attended a Catholic Mass, you would see and hear the Old and the New combined in such a way no other church combines them. The Mass is saturated with Sacred Scripture and Sacred Tradition...

Leviticus 7:12-15a, "When anyone makes a peace offering in thanksgiving, together with his thanksgiving sacrifice he shall offer unleavened cakes mixed with oil, unleavened wafers spread with oil, and cakes made of fine flour mixed with oil and well kneaded. His offering shall also include loaves of leavened bread along with the victim of his peace offering for thanksgiving. From each of his offerings he shall present one portion as a contribution to the Lord; this shall belong to the priest

who splashes the blood of the peace offering. The flesh of the thanksgiving sacrifice shall be eaten on the day it is offered;"

Acts 2:42-43, "They devoted themselves to the teaching of the apostles and to the communal life, to the breaking of the bread and to the prayers. Awe came upon everyone, and many wonders and signs were done through the apostles."

The Todah Offering

Psalm 116:13-17, "I will raise the cup of salvation and call on the name of the Lord. I will pay my vows to the Lord in the presence of all his people. Too costly in the eyes of the Lord is the death of this faithful. Lord, I am your servant, your servant, your servant, the child of your maid-servant; you have loosed my bonds. I will offer a sacrifice of thanksgiving and call on the name of the Lord."

A Todah (or thanksgiving) sacrifice would be offered by someone whose life was delivered from great peril. The redeemed person would have his closest friends meet at the Temple for a Todah sacrificial meal. The priest would sacrifice the lamb in the Temple. The bread for the meal would be consecrated at the same moment the lamb was sacrificed. The sacred Todah meal would consist of bread, meat, and wine. Prayers and songs of thanksgiving would be said and sung. This is a Catholic Mass.

Another example of the Todah in the bible is **1 Chron. 16:2-3, "When David had finished offering up the holocausts and peace offerings, he blessed the people in the name of the Lord, and distributed to every Israelite, to every man and to every woman, a loaf of bread, a piece of meat, and a raisin cake."** David's offering was bread and meat for the sacrifice. Most significantly, David had the Levites lead the people. (**1 Chron. 16:8-36**). At this point in Israel's story, David not only changes the location of the ark, but Israel's liturgy is also transformed. The celebration that brought the ark into Jerusalem, the Todah, became the Levites primary job. They were to invoke, to thank, and to praise the LORD.

The Mass in Scripture:[2]

"The Old Testament: Foreshadowing the Mass

Throughout the Old Testament, we see signs of the Mass to come. The Mass didn't just appear out of nowhere: it stands at the end of a long story we call Salvation History.

---

[2] "The Mass in Scripture" excerpted from "Faith Charts: The Mass at a Glance" by Mike Aquilina ©Our Sunday Visitor. Used by permission, no other use of this material is authorized.

God's earliest people offered sacrifices to the Lord, both to atone for their sins and to give God thanks for His salvation.

Melchizedek, priest of God Most High, brought Abraham bread and wine. New Testament writers see Melchizedek as a foreshadowing of Christ (see **Hebrews 7**)

The Passover sacrifice foreshadowed the sacrifice of Christ, which saves us from death and bondage to sin. [The Passover, saved the Hebrew's firstborn children from death and ultimately was the final straw that released them from Egyptian slavery.]

The Law of Moses prescribed sacrificial rites for all Israel, again foreshadowing the perfect sacrifice of our Christian Mass.

The Psalms brought the Sacrifice of Thanksgiving to the fore --- a sacrifice that Greek-speaking Jews would know as 'the thanksgiving' (Eucharistia, from which we get 'Eucharist').

The prophet Malachi foretold a time when a pure sacrifice would be offered to the Lord all over the earth. **Malachi 1:11, 'For from the rising of the sun, even to its setting, My Name is great among the nations; And everywhere they bring sacrifice to My Name, and a pure offering; For great is My Name among the nations, says the Lord of Hosts.'**

New Testament: The Apostles Celebrate the Mass

Jesus Christ told His disciples that they must eat His flesh and drink His blood (**John 6:53-56**).

At the Last Supper, Christ instituted the Mass when He said 'This is my Body' and 'This is my Blood' (**Matthew 26:26-28**)

On the Road to Emmaus, Jesus' followers recognized Him in the breaking of the bread (**Luke 24:13-35**).

The Apostles celebrated the Mass with the very first Christians (**Acts 2:42**)

Before the Gospels were written down, St. Paul wrote an account of the Last Supper and gave the Corinthians instructions for celebrating the Mass (**1 Corinthians 11:23-34**)

The Letter to the Hebrews put the Mass in the context of salvation history.

Revelation showed how the Mass on earth is part of the worship that goes on constantly and forever in heaven."

So why don't Catholics bring their bibles to church? We don't bring our bibles to church because the church would be loud with the sound of flipping pages! We wouldn't be able to keep up! Our mass connects the old and the new. There is a reading from the Old Testament, a reading from the New

Testament, a Psalm (or a portion of one), and the Gospel. The awesome thing about it is the readings all connect with the same message or prophecy fulfilled. The mass was put together with such thought and devotion. It is beautiful.

Dr. Scott Hahn who was a Presbyterian. Dr. Hahn is extremely well versed in the bible. He was ordained a Presbyterian minister in 1982. After doing research on the Early Church Fathers, he wanted to know more about this "liturgy" the early church fathers spoke of so he attended a daily mass at a local Catholic church. Being so well versed in the bible, he was astounded at how much scripture was in the mass. He kept going to mass to learn more and has never stopped going. That was 39 years ago. He is now one of the biggest names in Catholic theology and apologetics. It was the mass that converted him. You can read his conversion story in his book called <u>The Lamb's Supper</u> by Scott Hahn.

The Early Christians on the Mass[3]

---

[3] "The Early Christians on the Mass" excerpted from "Faith Charts: The Mass at a Glance" by Mike Aquilina ©Our Sunday Visitor. Used by permission, no other use of this material is authorized.

"Christ said **'This is my Body'** and **'This is my Blood'** at the Last Supper (about 30 A.D.), and we can see, from the writings they left, that the early Christians believed His words. From the first generation on, they revered the consecrated bread and wine as the true Body and Blood of Christ. They saw the Mass as a true sacrifice, and Holy Communion as the sacrament that united the whole Church.

We should do all things in their proper order, which the Lord has commanded us to perform at the stated times. He has commanded offerings to be presented and services to be performed, not in a thoughtless or irregular way, but at the appointed times and hours.

-- St. Clement of Rome, To the Corinthians, about 90 A.D.

We do not receive these as common bread and drink. For Jesus Christ our Savior, made flesh by the Word of God, had both flesh and blood for our salvation. Likewise, we have been taught that the food blessed by the prayer of His Word -- and from which our own blood and flesh are nourished and changed -- is the flesh and blood of Jesus who was made flesh.

-- St. Justin Martyr, First Apology 66, about 155 A.D.

For the bread, which produced from the earth, is no longer common bread, once it has received the invocation of

God; it is then the Eucharist, consisting of two realities, earthly and heavenly.

-- St. Irenaeus of Lyons, Against Heresies 4.18.5, about 180 A.D."

What the Catechism says:

CCC 1343: It was above all on "the first day of the week," Sunday, the day of Jesus' resurrection, that the Christians met **"to break bread."** (**Acts 20:7**) From that time on down to our own day the celebration of the Eucharist has been continued so that today we encounter it everywhere in the Church with the same fundamental structure. It remains the center of the Church's life.

The Holy Spirit prepares for the reception of Christ CCC 1093: In the sacramental economy, the Holy Spirit fulfills what was prefigured in the Old Covenant. Since Christ's Church was "prepared in marvelous fashion in the history of the people of Israel and in the Old Covenant," (Lumen Gentium 2) the Church's liturgy has retained certain elements of the worship of the Old Covenant as integral and irreplaceable, adopting them as her own: -- notably, reading the Old Testament; -- praying the Psalms; -- above all, recalling the saving events and significant realities which have found their fulfillment in the mystery of Christ (promise and covenant, Exodus and Passover, kingdom and temple, exile, and return).

CCC 1096: <u>Jewish liturgy and Christian liturgy.</u> A better knowledge of the Jewish people's faith and religious life as professed and lived even now can help our better understanding of certain aspects of Christian liturgy. For both Jews and Christians Sacred Scripture is an essential part of their respective liturgies: in the proclamation of the Word of God, the response to this word, prayer of praise and intercession for the living and the dead, invocation of God's mercy. In its characteristic structure, the Liturgy of the Word originates in Jewish prayer. The Liturgy of the Hours and other liturgical texts and formularies, as well as those of our most venerable prayers, including the Lord's Prayer, have parallels in Jewish prayer. The Eucharistic Prayers also draw their inspiration from the Jewish tradition. The relationship between Jewish liturgy and Christian liturgy, but also their differences in content, are particularly evident in the great feasts of the liturgical year, such as Passover. Christians and Jews both celebrate the Passover. For Jews, it is the Passover of history, tending toward the future; for Christians, it is the Passover fulfilled in the death and Resurrection of Christ, though always in expectation of its definitive consummation.

CCC 1097: In the liturgy of the New Covenant every liturgical action, especially the celebration of the Eucharist and the sacraments, is an encounter between Christ and the Church. The liturgical assembly derives its unity from the "communion of the Holy Spirit" who gathers the children of God into the one Body of Christ. This assembly transcends racial, cultural, social -- indeed, all human affinities.

~ The Crucifix ~

The crucifix is an essential to our faith because it reminds us that I put Him on that cross. My sins nailed Him to that cross. But here is where Jesus mentions the crucifix in the bible...

We all know the verse **John 3:16**, but what does **John 3:14-15** say? Once again, we have to go back to the Old Testament first -- as it should be -- before we go to the New. Every fabric is connected. You cannot understand the New without the Old.

Numbers 21:4-9, "From Mount Hor they set out by way of the Red Sea, to bypass the land of Edom, but the people's patience was worn out by the journey; so the people complained against God and Moses, 'Why have you brought us up from Egypt to die in the wilderness, where there is no food or water? We are disgusted with this wretched food!' So the Lord sent among the people saraph serpents, which bit the people so that many of the Israelites died. Then the people came to Moses and said, 'We have sinned in complaining against the Lord and you. Pray to the Lord to take the serpents from us.' So Moses prayed for the people, and the Lord said to

Moses, 'Make a saraph and mount it on a pole, and if anyone who has been bitten looks at it, he will recover.' Moses accordingly made a bronze serpent and mounted it on a pole, and whenever anyone who had been bitten by a serpent looked at the bronze serpent, he recovered."

And now we can fast forward to the New Testament when Jesus is talking to Nicodemus in **John 3:14-15, "And just as Moses lifted up the serpent in the desert, so must the son of man be lifted up, so everyone who believes in Him may have eternal life."** Wouldn't we all agree the bite by the serpent is a representation of sin? Looking at a crucifix brings many to repentance.

If you have ever stared at a crucifix, you understand why it is an essential part of our faith. I remember a time when I sat and stared at a crucifix for a good long, and the overwhelming thoughts of what happened that day rushed through my head. It was such a revelation! What dawned on me was His crown was still on His Head as He was dying on the cross. They were still mocking Him even as He died. I would never have experienced or reflected on that if I hadn't had that tangible image before me.

Jesus gave us the image of His Face on the shroud of Turin, and **He says, "He who has seen Me has seen the Father."** He gave us His image to adore. Stephen Ray, another convert to the Catholic faith, spoke about how he always thought Catholics were blasphemers and idolaters for worshiping an "image" of God. Then one day, it hit him like a ton of bricks. Protestants also depict Jesus to look just like we do. He is in Protestant paintings and children's books. It's the same face we have on the cross. The crucifix is a reminder of the Ultimate Sacrifice He made for us.

What the Catechism says:

Jesus consummates His sacrifice on the Cross CCC 616: It is love "**to the end**" (**John 13:1**) that confers on Christ's sacrifice its value as redemption and reparation, as atonement and satisfaction. He knew and loved us all when He offered His life (**Gal. 2:20, Eph. 5:2, 25**). Now "**the love of Christ controls us, because we are convinced that one has died for all; therefore, all have died.**" (**2 Cor. 5:14**) No man, not even the holiest, was ever able to take on himself the sins of all men and offer himself as a sacrifice for all. The existence in Christ of the divine person of the Son, who at once surpasses and embraces all human persons and constitutes Himself as the Head of all mankind, makes possible His redemptive sacrifice for all.

CCC 617: The Council of Trent emphasizes the unique character of Christ's sacrifice as "**the source of eternal salvation**" (**Heb. 5:9**) and teaches that "His most holy Passion on the wood of the cross merited justification for us." (Council of Trent: DS 1529) And the Church venerates His cross as it sings: "Hail, O Cross, our only hope." (from Liturgy of the Hours, Lent, Holy Week, Evening Prayer, Hymn Vexilla regis.)

~ Honoring Mary ~

Genesis 3:15, "And I will put enmity between you and the woman, and between your offspring and her offspring; He shall bruise your head, and you shall bruise His heel." The "woman" God is speaking of is Mary. He already knows that it is her seed that will crush Satan's head. Satan despises Mary because it is through her humility and obedience to God that God's plan was fulfilled.

Some may say, "We worship a jealous God. Giving honor to Mary would make Him angry and jealous." My first snarky response to that is: God did not have a mother in the Old Testament. Many stories in the New Testament mentions Mary being there (a few examples are further in this chapter). If she wasn't significant, why was it significant to mention she was there? She was (and still is) a servant of God.

The fourth Commandment states, **"Honor thy father and mother."** Why wouldn't that Commandment apply to Jesus' own mother? I cannot love Mary more than Jesus loves her. In my opinion, many denominations are very disrespectful to the mother of our Lord and Savior.

Hundreds of years after Mary was assumed into Heaven, the Church concluded that Mary had to be conceived without original sin. Old Testament Scripture states God could not be near sin. Therefore, Mary had to be without original sin. She was (is) the Eve that said, "Yes" to God's Will, not her will.

A priest explained it in this way: "God had to have so much trust in Mary for Him to be completely defenseless and dependent on her." Really think about that. Jesus (God Incarnate) was formed and grew in her womb. His Blood exchanged with hers. They were one for nine months. He was born of a virgin. He <u>chose</u> Mary. Not just <u>any</u> woman could have been Mary. He knew who she was and exactly when she was going to play her part in His plan for salvation. Mary gave God His humanity -- His human form. She is the only person He could find rest and sanctuary in. Think about this also: During His birth, God gave her no material comforts to care for Him as a newborn babe -- God made flesh. He had complete and total trust in her.

This woman that God put His very life into her hands, who nourished Him, nurtured Him, loved Him, and raised Him deserves no honor? The mother that kissed His little hands and feet, the mother that wiped His tears, followed Him to Calvary and stayed at the foot of the cross where He was placed in her arms after being taken down from the cross deserves no honor? Should she just be considered an incubator? A vessel that God used and disposed of?

Even John the Baptist leaped in his mother's womb at the sound of her voice. **Luke 1:41-42, "When Elizabeth heard Mary's greeting, the infant leaped in her womb, and Elizabeth, filled with the Holy Spirit, cried out in a loud voice and said, 'Most blessed are you among women, and blessed is the fruit of your womb.'"** Those words that Elizabeth said are the very same words we say in the Hail Mary prayer, **"Blessed are you among women, and blessed is the fruit of your womb."** And Mary then replies with her Magnificat, her Psalm, **"Nations will call me blessed... Holy is His Name."** (Luke 1:46-55)

<u>Mary is the Living Ark of the Covenant</u>

2 Samuel 6:9, "David feared the Lord that day and said, 'How can the ark of the Lord come to me?'"

2 Samuel 6:11, "The ark of the Lord remained in the house of Obededom the Gittite for three months, and the Lord blessed Obededom and his whole house."

Luke 1:43, "Elizabeth said, 'And how does this happen to me, that the mother of my Lord should come to me?'"

Luke 1:56, "Mary remained with her about three months and then returned to her home."

It was no coincidence that Luke used this wording. He knew what and who he was referring to. The ark of the covenant contained a jar of manna (the bread sent from heaven to feed God's people in the desert), the 10 Commandments (the Word of God), and Aaron's staff (the High Priest) **Hebrews 9:3-4**. Mary, the ark of the New Covenant contained the Word made flesh, the Bread of Life, and the Priest of Priests. (Side Note: Another point to bring up about the eucharist: He is the Word made flesh AND the Bread of Life. Not meaning to consume just the Word. There is an actual Bread made flesh to consume.)

<u>To Jesus through Mary</u>

John 2:1-5, "On the third day there was a wedding in Cana in Galilee, and the mother of Jesus was there. Jesus and His disciples were also invited to the wedding. When the wine ran short, the mother of Jesus said to Him, 'They have no wine.' And Jesus said to her, 'Woman, how does your concern affect me? My hour has not yet come.' His mother said to the servers, 'Do whatever He tells you.'" We believe Jesus was acknowledging His mother's ability to intercede and by her disregarding His words, **"My hour has not yet come."** We believe it was on her cue that He began His public ministry. And what are Mary's last words spoken in the bible? **"Do whatever He tells you."** Her mission has always been to point everyone back to her Son. Like the moon in the night

sky, she does not emit her own light, but the sun (Son) illuminates her.

Mary, Queen of Heaven and Earth

Revelation 12:1-2, "A great sign appeared in the sky, a woman clothed with the sun, with the moon under her feet, and on her head a <u>crown of twelve stars</u>. She was with child and wailed aloud in pain as she labored to give birth." This verse is of course speaking of Mary, the mother of God, crowned with the stars of the heavens. As mentioned in the Magisterium chapter, all of God's creation has hierarchy and crowning her in Revelation was not to be misconstrued. John could have said **"stars above her head,"** or why even mention a crown of stars at all if it wasn't significant to the vision?

Mary is part of God's redemptive plan. Mary is a model of virtue for us and an intercessor for us as our spiritual mother. She leads us to her Lord and Savior, her son, Jesus Christ.

Mary, Our Intercessor

Just like the wedding in Cana, Mary brings our prayers and pleas to her Son. St. Louis DeMontfort says in his book:

<u>True Devotion to the Blessed Virgin Mary</u>:

"She enriches our good works by adorning them with her own merits and virtues. It is as if a poor peasant, wishing to win the friendship and favour of the king, were to go to the queen and give her an apple - his only possession - for her to offer it to the king. The queen, accepting the peasant's humble gift, puts it on a beautiful golden dish and presents it to the king on behalf of the peasant. The apple in itself would not be a gift worthy of a king, but presented by the queen in person on a dish of gold, it becomes fit for any king.

Mary presents our good works to Jesus. She does not keep anything we offer for herself, as if she were our last end, but unfailingly gives everything to Jesus. So by the very fact we give anything to her, we are giving it to Jesus. Whenever we praise and glorify her, she sings today as she did on the day Elizabeth praised her, **'My soul glorifies the Lord'**" [4]

John 19:26, "When Jesus then saw His mother, and the disciple whom He loved standing nearby, He said to His mother, 'Woman, behold, your son!' Then He said to the disciple, 'Behold, your mother.'" We have to ask ourselves if this is something Jesus would overlook? Making arrangements for His mother while He was dying on the cross? Nothing He said or did was null or void. Everything

---

[4] Total Consecration to Mary by Louis DeMontforte Pg. 68-69 No. 147 & 148

He did had meaning. Deep meaning. **"Whoever has ears ought to hear."**

Mary is but a humble servant to her Son. She wants nothing more than for everyone to return to her Son, the Most High God. When she said, "Yes" to God she became the daughter of the Father, the mother of the Son, and the spouse of the Holy Spirit. She is the only human being to hold those titles forever. She will always point us to God.

Mary is God's Masterpiece

One of the oldest cave drawings in the catacombs in Rome is a drawing -- or carving -- of the Madonna and Child. She is the most painted woman in history. Many Renaissance Artists and earlier paintings, murals, and sculptures of our Blessed Mother and the Christ Child. Wolfgang Mozart, Ludwig Beethoven, Johann Christian Bach, and many other composers wrote Symphonies for her. Yet she does not take any of these things for herself. It is all given back for the glory of her Son, our Lord and Savior, Jesus Christ.

"She who first gave Him to the world will establish His Kingdom in the world."[5]

Marian Apparitions

---

[5] Total Consecration to Mary by Louis DeMontforte Pg. 6

There is so much to say about Marian Apparitions and the messages she has given us over the past hundreds of years, but I will try to keep it brief by giving you just a small list of apparitions that left behind miraculous, unexplainable relics, images, etc.

<u>Our Lady of Guadalupe in Mexico</u> - In 1531 Our Lady appeared to St. Juan Diego. On her last visit, she had him pick roses in the desert, which was very unusual because it was December and it was the desert. He brought them to her and she arranged them in his tilma and told him to bring it to the bishop. When he went before the bishop, he opened his tilma to reveal a beautiful image of the Blessed Mother. His tilma is still on display today in the Shrine that was built on the spot St. Juan Diego saw Our Lady. I encourage you to look up the miracles and the history of that tilma! There are so many incredible mysteries with the tilma. I can write a whole book on just that! The amazing thing about this apparition was this apparition took place during the Spanish and Aztec war, which brought millions together from both sides. But it also took place in Mexico at the same time Martin Luther was breaking away from the church in England. So, Our Blessed Mother was replenishing the flock at the same time it was being diminished in England.

<u>Our Lady of Las Lajas in Columbia</u> - In 1754 Maria Mueses and her deaf-mute daughter Rosa discovered an

image of Our Lady and the child Jesus on the rock on the side of a mountain. Rosa was cured and there is much more to the story, but the miraculous image is still there today. People have drilled into the image to take a piece for testing and discovered that the image imprints in the rock several feet deep! They built a beautiful church against the side of the mountain, framed out the image and built the altar right below the image.

<u>Our Lady of Lourdes in France</u> - In 1858 Our Lady appeared to St. Bernadette Sourbirous (pronounced like the car Subaru). During one of the apparitions, Mary told her to dig in the dirt and eat it. St. Bernadette did so. People laughed at her and called her crazy. Soon after, a spring of water came up from where St. Bernadette dug. That spring is still there today and heals many many people who come to it.

And of course, the Marian Apparition to the 3 children in Fatima:

<u>Our Lady of Fatima in Portugal</u> - In 1917 she appeared to 3 children over the course of 6 months. From May to October, on the 13th of every month. On October 13th, 1917, a miracle happened in the sky. Approximately 70,000 people were there on that very rainy, wet day. After Our Lady appeared and spoke to the children, she pointed to the sun. The sun danced in the sky then appeared to plummet toward earth. The people were terrified. The sun then went back to

its normal position and all the people were bone dry. The ground, their clothing, everything was completely dry. It was the year 1917 so there were newspapers and photos at the time. You can look this up for yourself to read about that incredible miracle.

We Catholics have been keeping a very close eye on the apparition in Fatima and quite a few others. Much of what is happening right now is being connected to the messages she told the children back then. I encourage you to take a deeper look into all of these apparitions.

What the Catechism says:

CCC 2617: Mary's prayer is revealed to us at the dawning of the fullness of time. Before the Incarnation of the Son of God, and before the outpouring of the Holy Spirit, her prayer cooperates in a unique way with the Father's plan of loving kindness: at the Annunciation, for Christ's conception; at Pentecost, for the formation of the Church, his Body. (**Luke 1:38; Acts 1:14**) In the faith of His humble handmaid, the Gift of God found the acceptance He has awaited from the beginning of time. She whom the Almighty made "**full of grace**" responds by offering her whole being: "**Behold I am the handmaid of the Lord; let it be [done] to me according to your word.**" "Fiat": this is Christian prayer: to be wholly God's, because He is wholly ours.

CCC 2675: Beginning with Mary's unique cooperation with the working of the Holy Spirit, the Churches developed their prayer to the holy Mother of God, centering it on the person of Christ manifested in His mysteries. In countless hymns and antiphons expressing this prayer, two movements usually alternate with one another: the first "magnifies" the Lord for the "great things" He did for His lowly servant and through her for all human beings (**Luke 1:46-55**); the second entrusts the supplications and praises of the children of God to the Mother of Jesus, because she now knows the humanity which, in her, the Son of God espoused.

~ The Angels & Saints ~

~ The Church Triumphant ~

When our children are active in sports, dance, or music, we point them to people who were successful in that skill or talent. Unfortunately, most role models in most professions that we point our children to are not the most righteous of people. These "role models" are usually quite the opposite of righteous or upright.

<u>Saints point to God</u>

Lives of the Saints are reminders of how to live a Holy life. Every Saint has a story of their struggles, their extreme obedience to God, and their faith journey on this earth. Many Saints lived a good part of their lives with little to no faith. Some struggled with addictions, some persecuted Christians before they found themselves at the foot of the cross completely submitting themselves to His Holy Will. Catholics have Saint statues that are relatable to their struggles. Saints remind us that no matter how hard the struggle may be, we can do it. **Hebrews 12:1-2b, "Therefore, since we are** surrounded by so great a cloud of witnesses, let us rid ourselves of every burden and sin that clings to us and persevere in running the race that lies before us while keeping our eyes fixed on Jesus, the leader and perfecter of faith."

Communion of Angels and Saints

Genesis 28:12, "Then he [Jacob] had a dream: a stairway rested on the ground, with its top reaching to the heavens; and God's messengers were going up and down on it."

Saints are not to be worshiped, they are examples and reminders of what kind of relationship we should have with God. They are also prayed to for their intercession. They have lived their lives for God, striving to please only Him. Like Noah, Moses, Elijah, Elisha, Jeremiah, and all the other Old Testament prophets, they are mediators. They were the ones who found favor with God and interceded for the people and most importantly, they are great examples of being human. Why didn't the Jews pray to the prophets? Because the gates of heaven were not yet opened. They "went to sleep with their ancestors" (**1 Kings 2:10, 2 Peter 3:4**)

Romans 12:4-5, "Just as each of us has one body with many members, and these members do not all have the

same function, so in Christ we who are many form one body, and each member belongs to all the others."

Those united in Christ are united to one another. We ask others to pray for us. Paul asks in **Romans 15:30, "I urge you, brothers, by our Lord Jesus Christ and by the love of the Spirit, to join me in my struggle by praying to God for me." Hebrews 13:18**

Why wouldn't we seek for the intercession of those who have gone before us?

John 15:5, "I am the vine, you are the branches. Whoever remains in me and I in him will bear much fruit, because without me you can do nothing." We are all branches on the vine. We are only cut off from the vine if we do not remain in Him. (**John 15:6**). The saints are branches of the vine of Jesus Christ in heaven. The followers of Christ are the branches on earth, and we are encouraged to intercede for one another. That being the case, why wouldn't the saints, who are still branches of the vine, intercede for the followers of Christ on earth as well? The saints in heaven pray for the saints on earth.

Just like a person would seek guidance and support from someone who has gone through a similar situation we are dealing with, we tend to pray to the saint who dealt with similar struggles of our own and overcame those struggles through Christ.

The angels intercede for us by bringing the prayers of the faithful before the throne of our Father: **Revelation 5:8, "And when he had taken it [the scroll], the four living creatures and the twenty-four elders fell down before the Lamb. Each one had a harp and they were holding golden bowls full of incense, which are the prayers of the saints."**

And again, **Revelation 8:3-4 - 'Another angel, who had a golden censer, came and stood at the altar. He was given much incense to offer, with the prayers of all the saints, on the golden altar before the throne. The smoke of the incense, together with the prayers of the saints went up before God from the angel's hand.'"**

The angels, Mary, and the saints are our heavenly helpers. We acknowledge that the angels, who are spirits created by God, assist us in our lives. We have a Guardian Angel to whom we can ask for help and guidance through the day and night. And we honor Mary and the saints as the holy men and women who have gone before us. But their intercession is completely dependent on the power of God.

We must remember, that the spiritual battle affects every part of our lives. As members of our spiritual family, when faced with the temptations of the world, the flesh, and the devil; we should use the power of God to call on the legion of angels and saints to help us with our daily struggles.

Paul says: **Ephesians 6:12 - 'For our struggle is not against the flesh, and blood, but against the rulers, against the authorities, against the powers of this dark world and against the spiritual forces of evil in the heavenly realms.'**

Another passage from Revelation, that will be repeated in the Purgatory chapter, **Revelation 7:9, "After this I had a vision of a great multitude, which no one could count, from every nation, race, people, and tongue. They stood before the throne and before the Lamb, wearing white robes and holding palm branches in their hands."**

Venerating Relics

Venerate means to regard highly, to give something (or someone) honor. The Hall of Fame, as I mentioned earlier in this chapter, is filled with "role models," people who accomplished something with their God-given talent, and most people who are venerated in the Hall of Fame are not very savory characters. Heaven has a Hall of Fame too. They are the "role models" of the church who won the race. Like the Hall of Fame would have the guitar from the hip-swinging, blues-y, jazz singer with the fabulous hair or the infamous round sunglasses from one of the 4 band members of the legendary English band that swept the nation; we have relics from the saints. Articles of clothing, replicas of their rooms or the homes they lived in, etc.

Acts 5:15-16, "Thus they even carried the sick out into the streets and laid them on cots and mats so that when Peter came by, at least his shadow might fall on one or another of them. A large number of people from the towns in the vicinity of Jerusalem also gathered, bringing the sick and those disturbed by unclean spirits, and they were all cured."

Acts 19:11-12, "So extraordinary were the mighty deeds God accomplished at the hands of Paul that when face cloths or aprons that touched his skin were applied to the sick, their diseases left them and the evil spirits came out of them."

There are relics of the martyred saints in the altars of the Catholic church because of all the verses mentioned above and also **Revelation 6:9, "When he broke open the fifth seal, I saw underneath the altar the souls of those who had been slaughtered because of the witness they bore to the work of God."**

Many denominations have lost so much of the teachings of our early church fathers because they dismiss the Catholic faith. If you go back before the 16th century -- before Martin Luther -- much of the writings and paintings were Catholic. St. Thomas Aquinas (late 1200s), St. Augustine

(400s), St. Jerome (400s), St. Polycarp (late 100s), Pope St. Clement I (late 100s) and so many more. They were all members of, or part of the magisterium, of the Catholic church. If we can look to Billy Graham for his wisdom in the past, why wouldn't we look to the wise men who walked with the apostles and their students?

As for my children, I would much rather them have an image or statue of a saint than a poster or picture of an athlete, actor, or musician of today. Through the saints, we, and our children, can learn how to live virtuous and pious lives.

Wouldn't we all agree we need a little bit more virtue and piety in our world today?

What the Catechism says:

CCC 2113: Idolatry not only refers to false pagan worship. It remains a constant temptation to faith. Idolatry consists of divinizing what is not God. Man commits idolatry whenever he honors and reveres a creature in place of God, whether this be gods or demons (for example, satanism), power, pleasure, race, ancestors, the state, money, etc. Jesus says, "**You cannot serve God and mammon.**" (**Mt 6:24**) Many martyrs died for not adoring "the Beast" (Cf. **Rev 13-14**) refusing even to simulate such worship. Idolatry rejects the unique Lordship of God; it is therefore incompatible with communion with God. (Cf. **Gal 5:20; Eph 5:5**)

CCC 2132: The Christian veneration of images is not contrary to the first commandment which proscribes idols. Indeed, "the honor rendered to an image passes to its prototype," and "whoever venerates an image venerates the person portrayed in it." (St. Basil, De Spiritu Sancto 18, 45; PG 32, 149C; Council of Nicea II: DS 601; cf. Council of Trent: DS 1821-1825; Vatican II Council: SC 126; Lumen gentium 67) The honor paid to sacred images is a "respectful veneration," not the adoration due to God alone.

~ Purgatory ~

~ The Church Suffering ~
"Nothing impure can enter Heaven." Rev. 21:27

So, we pray for the intercession of the Saints who made it to heaven, and we also pray for the souls that are in Purgatory. Jesus' second coming is when He comes to **"judge the living and the dead" 1 Peter 4:5, "but they will give an account to him who stands ready to judge the living and the dead."** Then he goes on to say in **verse 6, "For this is why the gospel was preached even to the dead that, though condemned in the flesh in human estimation, they might live in the spirit in the estimation of God."** So, he's talking about dead in spirit, right? But he's also talking about the living. **"He will come to <u>judge the living</u> and the dead."** It is in the Apostles Creed. If all of the faithful make it to heaven right away when they die, why would there be a second coming and a judgment of the living and the dead? Is the second coming only for the people who have not left their life on earth yet? **2 Timothy 4:1, "I charge you in the presence of God and of Christ Jesus,**

who will judge the living and the dead, and His appearing and His kingly power..."

Purgatory - the Place - in the Bible

In **2 Timothy 1:18,** Paul is praying for and asking Timothy to pray for Onesiphorus, a friend who passed away: **"May the Lord grant him to find mercy from the Lord on that day."** What day is Paul speaking of? --The day when Jesus comes to judge the living and the dead. We believe Paul is saying that Onesiphorus is not with Jesus yet, and he prays he will find mercy "on that day."

Revelation 7:9 speaks of the Saints who have made it to heaven: **"After this I had a vision of a great multitude, which no one could count, from every nation, race, people, and tongue. They stood before the throne and before the Lamb, wearing white robes and holding palm branches in their hands."** So, there are people who live a very pious and devout life that made it through the purification/Purgatory and were given their white robes.

We believe Purgatory is not a happy place. It's a place where we long to be with God, but having to be purified for a time to cleanse our souls from the stains of sin before we can enter heaven. **Zechariah 13:8, "In all the land, says the Lord, two thirds of them shall be cut off and perish, and** one third shall be left. I will bring the one third through fire, and I will refine them as silver is refined, and I will test them as gold is tested. They shall call upon my name, and I will hear them. I will say, 'They are my people,' and they shall say, 'The Lord is my God.'" We believe the one-third that does not perish but has to go through some kind of refinery/purification before they enter the kingdom of God. We believe this purification is Purgatory.

Yes, Jesus came to die for our sins. He did. Before Jesus, no one could enter the kingdom of heaven. After Jesus, the gates were opened, but our sinful souls still have to be cleansed before entering. That is where Purgatory comes in. **Rev. 21:27, "Nothing impure will ever enter it, nor will anyone who does what is shameful or deceitful, but only those whose names are written in the Lamb's book of life."** Those whose names are written in the Lamb's book still have to be purified before entering. **Revelation 20:12-13, "I saw the dead, the great and the lowly, standing before the throne, and scrolls were opened. Then another scroll was opened, the book of life. The dead were judged according to their deeds, by what was written in the scrolls. The sea gave up its dead; then Death and Hades gave up their dead. All the dead were judged according to their deeds."** If the souls in the Book of Life were already in heaven, why was it opened at the end of time? And if these dead St. John speaks of are already condemned souls, what need is there of judgment? Aren't they already judged? There seems to be a waiting period.

What the Catechism says:

CCC 1030: All who die in God's grace and friendship, but are still imperfectly purified, are indeed assured of their eternal salvation; but after death, they undergo purification, to achieve the holiness necessary to enter the joy of heaven.

CCC 1031: The Church gives the name "Purgatory" to this final purification of the elect, which is entirely different from the punishment of the damned. The Church formulated her doctrine of faith in Purgatory, especially at the Councils of Florence and Trent. The tradition of the Church, by reference to certain texts of Scripture, speaks of a cleansing fire: (Referencing to **1 Corinthians 3:15, "But if someone's work is burned up, that one will suffer loss; the person will be saved, but only as through fire."** and 1 Peter 1:7, **"so that the genuineness of your faith, more precious than gold that is perishable even though tested by fire, may prove to be for praise, glory, and honor at the revelation of Jesus Christ."**)

As for certain lesser faults, we must believe that, before the Final Judgement, there is a purifying fire. He who is truth says that **"whoever utters blasphemy against the Holy Spirit will be pardoned neither in this age nor in the age to come."** From this sentence, we understand that certain offenses can be forgiven at this age, but certain others in the age to come (**Matthew 12:32**).

CCC 1032: This teaching is also based on the practice of prayer for the dead, already mentioned in Sacred Scripture: **2 Maccabees 12:46 "Therefore [Judas Maccabeus] made atonement for the dead, that they might be delivered from their sin."** From the beginning, the Church has honored the memory of the dead and offered prayers in suffrage for them, above all the Eucharistic sacrifice, so that, thus purified, they may attain the beatific vision of God. The Church also commends almsgiving, indulgences, and works of penance undertaken on behalf of the dead:

Let us help and commemorate them. If Job's sons were purified by their father's sacrifice (**Job 1:5**), why would we doubt that our offerings for the dead bring them some consolation? Let us not hesitate to help those who have died and to offer our prayers for them.

~ The Rapture or Not ~

Matthew 24:40-44, "Two men will be out in the field; one will be taken, and one will be left. Two women will be grinding at the mill; one will be taken and one will be left. Therefore, stay awake! For you do not know on which day your Lord will come. Be sure of this: if the master of the house had known the hour of the night when the thief was coming, he would have stayed awake and not let his house be broken into. So too, you also must be prepared, for at an hour you do not expect, the Son of Man will come." And when He comes, what will He do? Is He saying He is the thief? Or should we always be prepared for the thief? I think the question is who is the thief? In the verses right before this, He speaks about Noah's time, **Matthew 24:38-39, "In [those] days before the flood, they were eating and drinking, marrying and giving in marriage, up to the day that Noah entered the ark. They did not know until the flood came and carried them all away."**

Then He goes on to say verse **24:40 "Two men will be out in the field..."** So, who is taken or "carried away"? It is not quite clear who exactly are the ones taken in 24:40. The good or the bad. But if He references to Noah and the bad being carried away, then says one will be taken, then goes on to say a thief in the night... it sounds like, if deeply reflected upon, it is the bad that will be taken.

In the parable of the faithful and the unfaithful servant that follows **Matthew 24:44**, it is the evil servant who is "sent" somewhere, **Matthew 24:48, "But if the wicked servant says to himself, 'My master is long delayed,' and begins to beat his fellow servants, and eat and drink with drunkards, the servant's master will come on an unexpected day at an unknown hour and will punish him severely and assign him a place with the hypocrites, where there will be wailing and grinding of teeth."** Even the goats who are separated from the sheep are the ones who are thrown into the fire. **Luke 3:9 and Matthew 3:10, "Therefore, every tree that does not bear good fruit is cut down and thrown into the fire." Matthew 18:8b, "it is better for you to enter life crippled or lame, than to have two hands or two feet and be thrown into everlasting fire."** Again, scripture from the last chapter, **Zechariah 13:8, "In all the land, says the Lord, two thirds of them shall be cut off and perish, and one third shall be left."** We believe it is the bad who are taken, carried, sent, or thrown somewhere.

But what about the parable of the ten virgins? The key phrase that begins that parable is **"Then the kingdom of heaven will be like..."** or in other translations, **"At that time, the kingdom of heaven will be like..."** (Matthew 25:1) When He comes again, He is uprooting the evil and bringing heaven down to earth to make a new Jerusalem. **Revelation 21:1-4, "Then I saw a new heaven and the former earth had passed away, and the sea was no more. I also saw the holy city, a new Jerusalem, coming down out of the heaven from God, prepared as a bride adorned for her husband. I heard a loud voice from the throne saying, 'Behold, God's dwelling is with the human race. He will dwell with them and they will be His people and God himself will always be with them [as their God]. He will wipe every tear from their eyes, and there shall be no more death or mourning, wailing or pain, [for] the old order has passed away.'"** That is the Church's wedding day.

The Catechism does not have anything on the rapture because it is not a Catholic belief or teaching of the Church.

The Church & Her Imagery

When you walk into a devout Catholic home, you know we are Catholic because of the imagery around our house. You know we follow Jesus and we honor His mother and seek guidance from those who have gone before us. Most of our churches are adorned in splendor because the True Presence of Our Lord Jesus Christ dwells in the Tabernacle. (See Chapter 1 - The Eucharist)

God created us with 6 senses (which includes spiritual). We use them all in our church. Why would He frown upon us using all of our senses to worship Him? The temple in the Old Testament shows God approving of imagery, honor, reverence, and splendor: God Himself instructed Moses in **Exodus 25:18-22, "Make two cherubim of beaten gold for the two ends of the cover; make one cherub at one end, and the other at the other end, of one piece with the cover, at each end. The cherubim shall have their wings spread out above, sheltering the cover with them; they shall face each other, with their faces looking toward the cover. The cover you shall then place on top of the ark. In the ark itself you are to put the covenant which I will give you. There I will meet between the two cherubim on the ark of the covenant, I will tell you all that I** command you regarding the Israelites." In Exodus 26:1, "The tabernacle itself you shall make out of ten sheets woven in fine linen twined and of violet, purple, and scarlet yarn, with cherubim embroidered on them." Exodus 26:31, "You shall make a veil woven of violet, purple, and scarlet yarn, and of fine linen twined, with cherubim embroidered on it." These are statues and images God wanted on and throughout His Temple. These were not gravening images to worship. Did the High Priest go into the Holy of Holies and worship the cherubim statues on the arc of the covenant? No, the cherubim were a reminder of who to worship. They point to God.

God loves imagery! Just take a look at the world. Let's take a look at the colors of the first temple. He requests violet, purple, and scarlet. The Israelites were <u>in the desert in biblical times</u>! Making bold colors was not an easy task. Purple was a color of royalty because of how hard it was to make in the Ancient World. I don't know what the difference is between violet and purple, but because He said two different shades of purple, they had to acquire two different shades of purple, which was not an easy task nor a cheap task either.

<u>God Wants Our Best</u>

Solomon's Temple was glorious and extravagant. God deserves splendor and awe in His house. He loves imagery! He loves it when we create for Him when we praise Him with our talents when we honor Him with the money He provides for us. When God speaks of tithing, there is a collection to be made from the community for the temple and priests, then from that collection, the priests are to take the best part of the gifts and give them to God, **Numbers 18:28-32, "Thus you too shall make a contribution from all the tithes you receive from the Israelites, handing over to Aaron the priest the part to be contributed to the Lord. From all the gifts that you receive, <u>and from the best parts</u>, you are to consecrate to the Lord your own full contribution.**

"Tell them also: Once you have made your contribution from the best part, the rest of the tithes will be credited to you Levites as if it were produce of the threshing floor or of the wine press. Your families, as well as you, may eat them anywhere, since they are your recompense for service at the meeting tent. You will incur no guilt so long as you make a contribution <u>of the best part</u>. Do not profane the sacred gifts of the Israelites and so bring death on yourselves." God wants the best from us. **Genesis 4:4, "while Abel, for his part,**

brought one of the <u>best</u> firstlings of his flock." Abel gave his best.

The Order Inside a Catholic Church

Exodus 40:21-30, "He [Moses] brought the ark into the Dwelling and hung the curtain veil, thus screening off the ark of the commandments, as the Lord had commanded him. He put the table in the meeting tent, on the north side of the Dwelling, outside the veil, and arranged the bread on it before the Lord, as the Lord had commanded him. He placed the lampstand in the meeting tent, opposite the table, on the south side of the Dwelling, and he set up the lamps before the Lord, as the Lord had commanded him. He placed the golden altar in the meeting tent, in front of the veil, and on it he burned fragrant incense, as the Lord commanded him. He hung the curtain at the entrance of the Dwelling. He put the altar of holocausts in front of the entrance of the Dwelling of the meeting, and offered holocausts and cereal offerings on it, as the Lord has commanded him. He placed the laver between the meeting tent and the altar, and put water in it for washing." If you are familiar with the inside of a Catholic church, the above verses sound very familiar. In a traditional Catholic church, the tabernacle is positioned in the east and the red light -- lampstand -- is to the right -- or south -- of the tabernacle.

More from Exodus (this verse was also used in the Magisterium chapter): **Exodus 28:40-41, "Likewise, for the glorious adornment of Aaron's sons you shall have tunics and sashes and turbans made. With these you shall clothe your brother Aaron and his sons. Anoint them and ordain them, consecrating them as my priests."** Of course, there were orphans and widows in the desert camps of the Israelites. But these garments and vestments were sacred and were to be made with the finest materials.

You might say, "But all that money spent in fancy extravagance could be given to the poor." **John 12:3-8, "Mary took a liter of costly perfumed oil made from genuine aromatic nard and anointed the feet of Jesus and dried them with her hair; the house was filled with the fragrance of the oil. Then Judas the Iscariot, one of his disciples, and the one who would betray him, said, 'Why was this oil not sold for three hundred days' wages and given to the poor?' He said this not because he cared about the poor but because he was a thief and held the money bag and used to steal the contributions. So, Jesus said, 'Leave her alone. Let her keep this for the day of my burial. You always have the poor with you, but

you do not always have me.'" Verse 6 tells us what type of person Judas was, but what Jesus says to him, **"You will always have the poor."** There will always be poor, oppressed, and enslaved people. Our journey is one of a fallen world. The Catholic church certainly has its human faults, but it also does an extreme amount of good with much of the money it receives all over the world. Many oppressed, poor, and enslaved people can find (and have found) refuge from the Catholic church.

I am certainly not saying we're perfect. I can hear the comments now about headlines, bad priests, personal experiences with the administration, etc. Just like Judas being one of the twelve, there was flaw and deceit in the very beginning, among the twelve. However, there is also much grace and goodness. It just depends on which you choose to look for.

Why do we put so much effort, time, and talent into our churches? It is because of the Eucharist (See Chapter 1).

What the Catechism says:

CCC 2134: The first commandment summons man to believe in God, to hope in Him, and to love Him above all else.

CCC 2135: **"You shall worship the Lord your God"** (**Mt. 4:10**). Adoring God, praying to Him, offering Him the worship that belongs to Him, fulfilling the promises and vows made to Him are acts of the virtue of religion which fall under obedience to the first commandment.

CCC 2141: The veneration of sacred images is based on the mystery of the Incarnation of the Word of God. It is not contrary to the first commandment.

~ Rote Prayers ~

~ The Church Militant ~

Deuteronomy 6:4-9, "Hear, O Israel! The Lord is our God, the Lord alone! Therefore, you shall love the Lord, your God, with all your heart, and with all your soul, and with all your strength. Take to heart these words which I enjoin on you today. Drill them into your children. Speak of them at home and abroad, whether you are busy or at rest. Bind them at your wrist as a sign and let them be as a pendant on your forehead. Write them on the doorposts of your houses and on your gates." Devout Catholics do exactly this. We recite prayers over and over. We drill them into our children's heads, we write them on our doorposts, we wear them on our wrists, and around our necks. Most of our prayers also exactly that: Loving the Lord our God with all our hearts, with all our souls, and with all our strength. I say "most" because we have other prayers that seek God's help or the intercession of a Saint through a struggle. But even in those prayers, we still adore and praise God.

Matthew 6:7-8, Jesus tells us not to babble on: **"'In praying, do not babble like the pagans, who think that they will be heard because of their many words. Do not be like them. Your Father knows what you need before you ask Him.'"** After He says this, He gives us the Our Father (or The Lord's Prayer) and says in **Matthew 6:9, "'<u>This is how you are to pray</u>: Our Father in heaven, hallowed by Your name, Your kingdom come, Your will be done, on earth as in heaven. Give us today our daily bread; and forgive us our debts, as we forgive our debtors; and do not subject us to the final test, but deliver us from the evil one.'"** Someone once said to me that Jesus says we should pray "like" this. But, I say, if your boss tells you to do your job "like" this, are you going to completely change it up or are you going to do your job the way your boss told you to? We're talking about God telling us to pray like this.

I don't understand why many denominations do not recite the Lord's Prayer. Jesus Himself instructed us to pray that prayer. Luke also makes an account of the Lord's Prayer in **Luke 11:2-4**.

And then He goes on to speak about persistent prayer in the following verses, **Luke 11:5-8, "And He said to them, 'Suppose one of you has a friend to whom he goes at midnight and says, 'Friend, lend me three loaves of**

bread, for a friend of mine has arrived at my house from a journey and I have nothing to offer him,' and he says in reply from within, 'Do not bother me; the door has already been locked and my children and I are already in bed. I cannot get up to give you anything.' I tell you, if he does not get up to give him the loaves because of their friendship, he will get up to give him whatever he needs because of his persistence.'" Rote prayers, when said from the heart, are very persistent and they seek the Will of God or help from a heavenly helper (referred to in the Angels & Saints Chapter).

Every devout Catholic, down to the youngest aged child, knows the Our Father, Hail Mary, and the Glory Be. Those are the three main prayers every Catholic child, in a devout household, is taught from when they are being formed in the womb.

We have chaplet prayers, litanies, deliverance prayers, rosaries, and more. The beautiful thing about them all is when we say them, we never say them alone. I am confident there are at least hundreds, maybe thousands, of others around the world praying that same prayer at the same time. My small voice becomes a megaphone up to heaven! **Matthew 18:20, "'For where two or three are gathered in my name, there am I in the midst of them.'"**

Many Catholics around the world also acknowledge the hour of Jesus's death at 3:00 pm every day. So, at 3 pm, many Catholics will pray the Chaplet of Divine Mercy followed by the rosary (see the prayer section at the end of the book for details), which between the 2 prayers takes a little under an hour. If you think about time zones, there is likely a 3:00 pm somewhere in the world a good part of the day and night. People are saying the Chaplet and the Rosary around the world for most of the 24 hours in the day. Together. I am thankful for the steady stream of prayers being repeated over and over again by Catholics. I could not imagine what this world would be like without those steady persistent prayers throughout every day and night.

This also happens every day in Mass. Every Catholic Church has the same mass around the world. Their readings may be different depending on the liturgical calendar they follow, but the mass and prayers in the mass are the same, every day around the world, a couple of times throughout the day. Talk about a megaphone to heaven from the four corners of the earth every day, 7 days a week/365 days a year!

Many Protestant churches close their doors all week. Some of them have services on Wednesday nights, but for the most part, their churches are only open on Sundays. The Catholic church gets attacked more frequently than any other church because, 1st: we do believe the Catholic church is <u>the</u>

<u>church</u> established by Jesus Christ here on earth, and that in itself gives reason for attack; and 2nd: because there are so many prayers and communion with God. As I said, I don't know where this world would be if it were not for the repeated prayers of the faithful Catholics throughout the world day and night, night and day.

<u>The Rosary</u>

We pray for Mary's intercession on our behalf. We are quoting scripture in the Hail Mary. The prayer begins with **Luke 1:28, "Hail Mary, full of grace, the Lord is with you,"** then we quote **Luke 1:42** when Elizabeth says, **"...blessed are you among women, and blessed is the fruit of your womb,"** we add His Name, Jesus in the prayer, then we finish the prayer with a petition for her intercession by saying, "Holy Mary, Mother of God, pray for us sinners, now and at the hour of our death. Amen." Which became the prayer said most frequently during the infamous plague called Black Death in England from 1347 - 1351.

The rosary is a petition to Our Blessed Mother in Heaven to pray for us. But we are also walking through the life of Jesus from St. Gabriel's visit to Mary through to His Ascension and beyond to Pentecost, the Assumption of Mary, and the Coronation of Mary:

The Joyful Mysteries: 1st: **Announcement from Gabriel to Mary** (aka the Annunciation), 2nd: **the Visitation with Mary and her cousin Elizabeth**, 3rd: **the Birth of Jesus** (aka the Nativity), 4th: **the Presentation of Jesus at the Temple**, and 5th: **the Finding of Jesus in the Temple when He was 12.**

The Sorrowful Mysteries: 1st: **the Agony in the Garden**, 2nd: **the Scourging at the Pillar**, 3rd: **Crowning of Thorns**, 4th: **Carrying of the Cross**, 5th: **the Crucifixion**.

The Glorious Mysteries: 1st: **Jesus' Resurrection**, 2nd: **His Ascension**, 3rd: **Pentecost**, 4th: Mary's Assumption, and 5th: The Crowning of Mary Queen of Heaven and Earth (Not biblical because Mary was still alive when the bible was being written.)

St. Pope John Paul II commissioned a 4th Mystery called
The Luminous Mysteries: 1st: **the Baptizing of Jesus by John the Baptist**, 2nd: **Jesus' First Public Miracle, the Changing of Water into Wine at the Wedding Feast in Cana**, 3rd: **Jesus' Proclamation that the Kingdom of Heaven is at Hand** (the beginning of Jesus' ministry), 4th: **the Transfiguration**, and 5th: **the Last Supper/Eucharist.**

You can listen to a rosary on whatever music app you have or you can watch one on the internet. There are beautiful scriptural rosaries with sacred images on the internet.

The Stations of The Cross

A beautiful way to spend Lent (the 40ish days before Easter) is to walk through the stations of the cross. Catholics will walk through the Stations at least once during Lent. Most Catholics will walk them on Good Friday. Some of us will walk them every day or every Wednesday and Friday. There are 14 stations from Jesus' arrest to His burial. A very moving devotion. Some of us will pray the Stations throughout the year and add the 15th station of His Resurrection. Some of us will pray the Stations throughout the year and add the 15th station of His Resurrection.

Chaplets

Chaplets are usually said on rosary beads; just different prayers are said on the beads. Some chaplets have their own smaller set of beads like the Sacred Heart of Jesus Chaplet, the Holy Face of Jesus Chaplet, and the St. Michael Chaplet just to name a few. But we typically repeat the same prayer on each bead until there is a break in the beads. There is usually one bead separate from the others and another prayer is said on that bead. Just another way to storm heaven.

Novenas

The word "novena" comes from the Latin word "novem," which means nine. There were ten days of Pentecost left after Jesus ascended to Heaven. Pentecost was the offerings made in the 50 days after the first Sabbath after Passover (**Leviticus 23:15-21**). Jesus appeared to them on Sunday, the first day beginning the 50 days of Pentecost and stayed in their midst for 40 days. He told them to wait in Jerusalem for **"the promise of the Father"** (**Acts 1:3b**) then He made His ascension to Heaven. They waited and prayed for nine days. On the 10th day, the day that marks the end of Pentecost, they received the Holy Spirit (**Acts: 2:1-4**)

Our novenas are specific prayers we say for nine consecutive days, or emergency novenas can be said for each hour for nine hours for one day. We then say a prayer of thanksgiving on the 10th day.

To say it again (no pun intended), all of these different prayers we memorize are prayers that we can confidently say. We are never saying them alone. I would estimate that hundreds to thousands of people worldwide are saying the same prayers I am saying at the same time I'm saying them, just like our mass. The same mass, the same prayers and the same readings are being said in all different languages every day around the world. That is what I call storming Heaven!

What the Catechism says:

CCC 2632: Christian petition is centered on the desire and search for the Kingdom to come, in keeping with the teaching of Christ (**Mt. 6:10, 33; Lk. 11:2,13**). There is a hierarchy in these petitions: we pray first for the Kingdom, then for what is necessary to welcome it and cooperate with its coming. This collaboration with the mission of Christ and the Holy Spirit, which is not that of the Church, is the object of the prayer of the apostolic community (**Acts 6:6, 13:3**). It is the prayer of Paul, the apostle par excellence, which reveals to us how the divine solicitude for all the churches ought to inspire Christian prayer (**Rom. 10:1; Eph. 1:16; Phil 1:9-11; Col. 1:3-6, 4:3-4, 12**). By prayer every baptized person works for the coming of the Kingdom.

CCC 2651: The tradition of Christian prayer is one of the ways in which the tradition of faith takes shape and grows, especially through the contemplation and study of believers who treasure in their hearts the events and words of the economy of salvation, and through their profound grasp of the spiritual realities they experience.

CCC 2669: The prayer of the Church venerates and honors the Heart of Jesus just as it invokes His most Holy Name. It adores the Incarnate Word and His Heart which, out of love for men, He allowed to be pierced by our sins. Christian prayer loves to follow the way of the cross in the Savior's steps. The stations from the Praetorium to Golgotha and the tomb trace the way of Jesus, who by His Holy Cross has redeemed the world.

CCC 2685: The Christian family is the first place of education in prayer. Based on the sacrament of marriage, the family is the "domestic Church" where God's children learn to pray "as the Church" and to persevere in prayer. For young children in particular, daily family prayer is the first witness of the Church's living memory as awakened patiently by the Holy Spirit.

~ Baptizing Our Babies ~

Why do we baptize our babies instead of waiting until they are old enough to make their own decision? My first question is: suppose they die before they make that decision? **John 3:5, "Jesus answered, 'Amen, amen, I say to you, <u>no one</u> can enter the kingdom of God without being born of water and Spirit.'"** Then Jesus tells His disciples in **Matthew 28:19, "'Go, therefore, and make disciples of all nations, baptizing them in the name of the Father, and of the Son, and of the Holy Spirit...'"** Paul reiterates in **Romans 6:3-4, "Or are you unaware that we who were baptized into Christ Jesus were baptized into His death? We were indeed buried with Him through baptism into death, so that, just as Christ was raised from the dead by the glory of the Father, we too might live in the newness of life."** We believe like the covenant God made with Abraham: **Genesis 17:12-14, "Throughout the ages, every male among you, when he is eight days old, shall be circumcised, including houseborn slaves and those acquired with money..." "If a man is uncircumcised..." "...such a one shall be cut off from his people; he has broken my covenant."**

Although our faith began with men and women being baptized, once the covenant is made, we are to do the same to our babies and new additions as adopted children

We believe we are born with original sin, but we are also very likely born into this world with spiritual attachments from our ancestors. Jesus removing the unclean spirit from the possessed boy: **Mark 9:21-22, "Then He questioned his father, 'How long has this been happening to him?' He replied, 'Since childhood. It has often thrown him into fire and into water to kill him...'"** We baptize our babies so they may receive that Grace from God immediately. To exorcize any spirit that may be attached at birth or soon after birth.

The covenant God made with Abraham: All the men, including children, in Abraham's house were to be circumcised. After that, the circumcision was to be done 8 days after the baby boy was born. **Acts 16:15, "After she [Lydia] and her household had been baptized, she offered us invitation,"** Her household was baptized because of her faith. **Acts 16:31-33, "And [to the jailer] they said, 'Believe in the Lord Jesus and you and your household will be saved.' So, they spoke the word of the Lord to him and to everyone in his house. He took them in at that hour of the night and bathed their wounds; then he and all his family were baptized at once."** "Believe in the

Lord Jesus and you and your household will be saved." It was through the master of the house's faith that his whole family was baptized and saved. Throughout the Bible, the parents are the blessings or the curses of their children. It is the parent's responsibility to baptize their children and raise their children on a firm faith foundation.

Truly, the only thing needed to be said is again, **John 3:5, "...no one can enter the kingdom of God without being born of water and Spirit."** Why risk 5, 7, 9 years of your child's life? What a tragedy if they never decide to get baptized or if something happens to them before they get baptized.

God gives us the authority as parents to raise our children in faith. It is ultimately the parent's decision to baptize their children. That decision should not be left up to the children. At a Catholic baby's baptism, the parents and Godparents both vow to raise this child in faith. Ultimately, we believe it is up to the upbringing of the child, but at least give them the graces they can only get through baptism to help them through.

What the Catechism says:

CCC 1250: Born with a fallen human nature and tainted by original sin, children also need the new birth in Baptism to be freed from the power of darkness and brought into the realm of the freedom of the children of God, to which all men are called (Council of Trent [1546]: DS 1514; **Col 1:12-14**). The sheer gratuitousness of the grace of salvation is particularly manifest in infant Baptism. The Church and the parents would deny a child the priceless grace of becoming a child of God were they not to confer Baptism shortly after birth (Codex Iuris Canonici, can. 867; Corpus Canonum Ecclesiarum Orientalium, cann. 681; 686, 1).

CCC 1251: Christian parents will recognize that this practice also accords with their role as nurturers of the life that God has entrusted them (Lumen gentium 11; 41; Gaudium et spes 48; Codex Iuris Canonici, can. 868).

CCC 1255: For the grace of Baptism to unfold, the parents' help is important. So too is the role of the godfather and godmother, who must be firm believers, able and ready to help the newly baptized -- child or adult -- on the road of Christian life (Codex Iuris Canonici, cann. 872-874). Their task is a truly ecclesial function (officum) (Sacrsanctum concilium 67). The whole ecclesial community bears some responsibility for the development and safeguarding of the grace given at Baptism.

~ My Conclusion ~

A Catholic friend of mine was once asked if Catholics are Christian. My friend chuckled and said, "<u>THE</u> Christian. We were the first!" (Thanks for that one Kate!) The word "Catholic" in Greek means universal. We are the Universal Church of Jesus Christ. We began with the apostles. Protestant denominations did not enter the scene until Martin Luther rebelled against the authority of the Catholic Church in the early 1500s.

There are over 1500 years of Salvation History before Protestantism was even a thing. The word "Protestant" was the name given to anyone who "protests against the papacy". As I have said in this book, good and bad will come and go. I will <u>not</u> leave the Church Jesus established here on earth, and I will certainly not leave it so bad guys can take it over. Imagine explaining that one on judgment day!

Since Martin Luther broke away, there are now thousands, maybe even tens of thousands of different Protestant denominations. Satan loves to tear apart and divide. But I did not put this book together to cause division, condemn, or dim anyone's belief. I wrote this because I seem to run into many different denominations that have a problem with Catholicism. And I think it's because they don't understand it. They don't understand why it's different from all the other denominations. They're afraid to accept anything or partake in prayers because they are unsure and assume it's blasphemous.

The Catholic faith is so rich and so deep. I learn more about it daily, and I pray I never reach a point of pride where I feel I know it all -- how sad it is for anyone who thinks that way. (Unfortunately, there are believers on both sides who think that way.)

I do know some Catholics who believe only Catholics can make it to heaven because we receive the Eucharist. I have also encountered Protestants who believe no Catholics are making it to heaven because we are idolaters and we "worship" Mary. I say we have no right to judge.

Matthew 7:1-2, "Stop judging, that you may not be judged. For as you judge, so will you be judged, and the measure with which you measure will be measured out to you."

But Are We Saved?

We're baptized, we receive the Eucharist, we say our prayers over and over again, we even have confession to clean our souls! So, are we saved? The answer simply put is maybe. It depends on the individual. We may check all the boxes our religion requires us to check but ultimately, it is up to you. Do you give your heart to Jesus every day? Are we letting Him mold us and change our wicked ways?

We can't just ask Jesus into our hearts and voila! we're saved. We are required to live a Christian life. To treat others with love, to feed the hungry, give drink to the thirsty, clothe the naked, counsel the ignorant, and pray for each other. We must seek to do God's Holy Will ("Fiat" means God's Will be done) every day. That is what a follower of Christ looks like.

A priest once said, "What's the difference between a saint and a sinner? The saint wakes up and tries again." We have to recognize our downfalls and keep trying to do better; to live a better day for Christ. We will fall into sin, but we can not take for granted God's mercy. His mercy did not come cheap and we should not treat it as such. We must wake up each day and try again.

He knows our hearts. We are a broken family in this broken world. We must come together under the banner of Jesus Christ, our Lord and Savior. **Mark 9:38-39, "'Teacher, we saw someone casting out demons in Your Name and we tried to prevent him because he was not following us.' But Jesus said, 'Do not hinder him, for there is no one who will perform a miracle in My Name, and be able to soon afterward to speak evil of Me.'"**

I am a Catholic who enjoys hearing how other denominations worship our Lord and Savior and would welcome a discussion anytime! I, of course, love talking about the beauty of my Catholic faith to anyone who is interested to hear.

There are far more fierce battles to be fought. We need to unite together under the banner of Jesus Christ. We must stop fighting amongst each other and unite the clans! May God Bless you and keep you. Thank you for taking the time to read this.

~ Catholic Prayers ~

<u>The Apostle's Creed</u>

I believe in God, the Father almighty, Creator of heaven and earth, and in Jesus Christ,

His only Son, our Lord, who was conceived by the Holy Spirit, born of the Virgin Mary,

suffered under Pontius Pilate, was crucified, died and was buried;

He descended into hell; on the third day, He rose again from the dead;

He ascended into heaven and is seated at the right hand of God the Father almighty; from there, He will come to judge the living and the dead.

I believe in the Holy Spirit, the Holy Catholic Church, the communion of saints, the forgiveness of sins, the resurrection of the body, and life everlasting. Amen

<u>Our Father</u>

Our Father, who art in Heaven, Hallowed be Thy Name.

Thy kingdom come, Thy will be done on earth as it is in Heaven.

Give us this day our daily bread and forgive us our trespasses, as we forgive those who trespass against us

And lead us not into temptation but deliver us from evil. Amen

Hail Mary

Hail Mary full of grace, the Lord is with you,
Blessed are you among women, and blessed is the fruit of your womb, Jesus. Holy Mary, Mother of God, pray for us sinners now and at the hour of death. Amen

Glory Be

Glory be to the Father, and to the Son, and the Holy Spirit; as it was in the beginning is now and ever shall be a world without end. Amen

The Fatima Prayer A prayer added to the rosary (Given to the children in Fatima whom Our Blessed Mother appeared - see the Honoring Mary chapter for more information.)
O My Jesus, forgive us our sins, save us from the fires of Hell.
Lead all souls to purgatory, especially those in most need of Thy mercy. Amen.

The Memorare

Remember, O most gracious virgin Mary that never was it known that anyone who fled to your protection, implored your help, or sought your intercession was left unaided. Inspired by this confident, O virgin of virgins, my Mother, to you do I come, before you I stand, sinful and sorrowful. O Mother of the Word Incarnate, despise not my petitions, but hear and intercede for them. Amen

The Angelus (Said 3 times a day: at 6am, 12pm, and 6pm)

    V. The Angel of the Lord declared unto Mary,

    R, And she conceived of the Holy Spirit.

    (Say the Hail Mary Prayer)

    V. Behold the handmaid of the Lord,

    R. Be it done unto me according to Thy Word.

    (Say the Hail Mary Prayer)

    V. And the Word was made flesh,

    R. (kneel, bow your head, make the sign of the cross, and say) And dwelt among us.

    (Say the Hail Mary Prayer)

    V. Pray for us O Holy Mother of God,

R. That we may be made worthy of the promises of Christ.

Let us pray. Pour forth we beseech Thee O Lord, Thy Grace into our hearts;

That we to whom the Incarnation of Christ Thy Son was made known by the message of an angel, may by His Passion and Cross be brought to the glory of His Resurrection. Through the same Christ Our Lord. Amen.

Saint Michael Prayer

Saint Michael the Archangel, defend us in battle.

Protect us from the snares of the devil. May God rebuke him, and I humbly pray.

And do thou, oh prince of heaven, cast into Hell satan and all the evil spirits.

Who prowl about the world seeking the ruin of souls. Amen

Guardian Angel Prayer

Oh, Angel of God, my Guardian dear,
To whom God's love commits me here.
Ever this day, be at my side
To light and guard,

To rule and guide. Amen.

Chaplet of Divine Mercy Prayers (Typically said at 3pm, at the hour of our Lord's death and said on rosary beads)

You expired, Jesus, but the source of life gushed forth for souls, and the ocean of mercy opened up for the whole world.

O font of Life, unfathomable Divine Mercy, envelop the whole world and empty Yourself upon us.

O Blood and Water which gushed forth from the Heart of Jesus as a font of mercy for us, I trust You.

O Blood and Water which gushed forth from the Heart of Jesus as a font of mercy for us, I trust You.

O Blood and Water which gushed forth from the Heart of Jesus as a font of mercy for us, I trust You

Said on the Our Father beads:

Eternal Father, I offer You the Body, Blood, Soul and Divinity of Your dearly beloved Son, our Lord Jesus Christ. I ask for atonement for our sins and those of the whole world.

Said on the Hail Mary beads:

For the sake of His sorrowful passion, Have mercy on us and on the whole world.

Final Prayers for the Divine Mercy Chaplet (after the 5th decade)

Holy God, Holy Mighty One, Holy Immortal One, have mercy on us and the world.

Holy God, Holy Mighty One, Holy Immortal One, have mercy on us and the world.

Holy God, Holy Mighty One, Holy Immortal One, have mercy on us and the world.

Eternal God, in Whom mercy is endless and the treasury of compassion inexhaustible, look kindly upon and increase Your mercy in us that in difficult moments, we may not despair nor become despondent but with great confidence submit ourselves to Your Holy Will, which is love and mercy itself. Amen.

O Greatly Merciful God, infinite Goodness, today, all mankind calls out from the abyss of its misery to Your Mercy, to Your Compassion, O God. And it is with its mighty voice of misery that it cries out. Gracious God, do not reject the prayers of this earth's exiles. O Lord, goodness beyond our understanding, Who are acquainted with our misery through and through and know that by our power, we cannot ascend to You. We implore You, anticipate us with Your Grace and keep on increasing Your Mercy in us that we may faithfully do Your Holy Will all through our life and at death's hour. Let the omnipotence of Your mercy shield us from the darts of our salvation's enemies that we may with confidence as Your children, await Your final coming. That day known to You alone, and we expect to obtain everything promised us by Jesus, in spite of all our wretchedness. For Jesus is our hope: through His Merciful Heart, as through an open gate, we pass through to heaven. Amen.

~ Resources ~

1. The New American Bible - St. Joseph edition
2. Catechism of the Catholic Church
3. Eucharistic Miracles of the World: www.eucharisticmiraclesoftheworld.org - website originally created by Blessed Carlo Acutis
4. Spiritual Warfare for Catholics by Fr. Jeffrey Steffon
5. www.turnbacktogod.com/the-story-of-the-todah/ written by Georgy
6. Great Adventure Bible Timeline Bible Study from Ascension Press
7. "What Changes?" "The Mass in Scripture," and "The Early Christians on the Mass" excerpted from "Faith Charts: The Mass at a Glance" by Mike Aquilina ©Our Sunday Visitor. Used by permission, no other use of this material is authorized.
8. Journey Through Scripture - Parousia - The Bible and the Mass Study from the St. Paul Center
9. A Biblical Walk Through the Mass by Edward Sri
10. The Lamb's Supper by Dr. Scott Hahn
11. Total Consecration to Mary by St. Louis DeMontforte

12.   Marian Consecration for Children by Carrie Gress

13.   The Order of Melchizadek by Fr. Kyle Schnippel - article from: www.catholicexchange.com

Made in the USA
Columbia, SC
17 October 2024